Poems

ISMENE COOK

ISBN 978-1-63784-495-3 (paperback)
ISBN 978-1-63784-496-0 (digital)

Hawes & Jenkins Publishing
16427 N Scottsdale Road Suite 410
Scottsdale, AZ 85254
www.hawesjenkins.com

Printed in the United States of America

Acknowledgements

Ismene Castle:
Even though they'll probably never get to read this I want to say that if it wasn't for my brother and sister I never would have started to write. Everyone needs that one person who opens that door to your dreams. Mine were my big brother and my little sister. So thanks for that. Also to the person who granted me Clarity. She is my rock.

This is a book of poems

Surprise, this is a book of poems,
I'll bet it's not what you expected;
But I'll be honest, at some point,
I might go back and make them connected.

Were you shocked to realize,
That I would change my story;
Did you try to memorize,
All my glory?

Did you try to envision,
A future with me;
Where my book was the best,
And maybe a movie?

Does this break your heart?
Does it make you cry?
Do you want to restart?
Or me to retry?

Here's the sad truth,
I quite like it this way,
See I told everyone this would be scary,
And now it's not.
You don't know what comes next,
So Surprise,
This is a book of poems.

Better

Dance like there's nobody watching,
And smile like you never cry,
And one day soon there will come a day,
Where you're name is all they can say.

Live like there's no tomorrow,
Like the end is coming soon,
And then take a bigger chance,
But continue to dance,
Because tonight girls we're gonna fight.

We're gonna play like it's our future,
And run like we're being chased,
Win like never before,
But never forget our way.

Because this moment right now,
Is the moment that we change,
We take the past and throw it out,
Because this time, it's our way.

We'll make our own mistakes,
Of that i'm completely sure,
But if we hold our heads high,
And try not to cry,
Then all that's left is to dance like there's nobody watching,
And continue to fight.

Fly

There is a fly on the wall,
That seems to know all;
It tells me secrets,
About all of ya'll.

There is a fly on the wall,
That continues to buzz;
I know it isn't right,
That we talk all night,
But it knows everything that was.

We discuss many things about you two,
About how you both should get a clue;
About that one time he saw you together,
Even though you swore on your life I was better.

So I've replaced you now,
I hope that causes you pain;
I hope you cry and whine, and have a cow,
Because you'll never have me again.

I have a fly,
A fly about 6'5;
Who knows me better,
Than you could ever.

Free Verse

This is a poem that I won't make rhyme,
Not because I don't know how,
Just because I don't feel like it,
I started this poem with a plan,
I've forgotten the plan so here I am,
I don't know where to go from here,
I've been making this up as I go,
I hope someday that someone will enjoy this,
Because I laughed as I wrote it,
So I've never wrote a poem like this,
How do you think I'm doing so far,
I hope you like it,
That you find it humorous,
Or laughed in the middle of class,
I hope that you're sitting in your seat,
With a smile on your face and,
A laugh in your throat and,
You say, this is a Free Verse I guess.

Sisters

Sisters are annoying of that I swear,
We call you names, play mean tricks, and pull your hair;
But we can be sweet as I'm sure you know,
We cuddle, give kisses, and keep you warm when you're cold.

Sisters aren't perfect, though our fathers disagree,
We mess up, we cry, and sometimes show greed;
But we try our hardest to be flawless,
We put on make-up, style our hair, and improve our knowledge.

Sisters have a future that we are taught to prepare,
To cook, to clean, and even to care;
But our use is not our own,
We aren't given a choice,
It's something we've been taught for years,
To hold children for boys.

Sisters are daughters who turn into lovers,
Lovers who then become someone's mother;
Mother's that teach their daughters,
Their fate as a sister is to grow into mothers too.

Start over

The fear I feel,
The pain I felt;
My ice cold heart,
You couldn't melt.

The times I cried,
Or didn't try;
I watched you fly,
When you died.

The bed feels cold,
Just like you told;
They said 'move on',
When you were gone.

I don't think they know,
I've lost my glow;
It's been buried down deep,
Because it's you I couldn't keep.

This isn't my best,
But it's a start;
I'll open with this,
Then open my heart.

Weak

I have a superpower,
But I'm kind of a coward;
See I live in a tower,
With a butler named Howard,
Who for some reason continues to glower;
Even though he's paid by the hour.

Tears

Though I do try,
Not to cry,
When I fly,
Through the sky,
At night,
My eyes,
Never stay dry,
So bye.

Here's your fear

My skin is crawling,
And my hair is standing up.
His blood is dripping,
The beast just growling.
My eyes are wide,
And my body shakes.
I can feel the fear,
Running through my veins.
His body just fell,
I heard it go splat.
I feel the blood,
As it lands on my face.
The beast comes forward,
This must be my end.
It just licked my face,
It can taste my tears,
As my body goes numb,
And my mind goes dumb,
All I can see is the top of its tongue.
As my mind goes dark,
I think of before,
Of all the things I love and adore.

I know

I'm 19 years old and I know what i want,
I'm not sure how to get it,
Or the path that i need,
But I do know i'm gonna be big.
I know of my future,
Of the plans I have made,
I know of the many risks,
That i'm sure to take.
I know there's a part of me,
Terrified to fail,
Just as I know of the part,
That doesn't give a hell,
So watch me climb,
And watch me cry,
Watch as I reach for the sky,
My future is bright,
Though only I see it,
I have faith,
And I know I can reach it,
My path is hard,
There are things in the way,
There are people who are fighting,
Keeping me at bay,
I won't give up,
I don't accept failure,
Though this is tough,
And I might lose your favor,
I'll earn it back,
There's no doubt about that,
Yes I complain,
I might even whine,
But I'll never give up on the life that is mine.

The people

There's people in the street who cry instead of eat.
There's kids at home who feel all alone.
There's women and children and men.
That I'm sure they need to mend.
There's students in class who can't stay awake,
But can't sleep at home for fear they won't wake.
These people are dying,
Being torn up inside,
But no one is helping,
We're letting them slide.
I won't allow this,
I won't step aside,
Because i know this is wrong,
And I'm starting to cry.
How can you watch,
And do nothing to help?
How could you do this?
Just listen to them yell!
I'm trying to change things,
Starting right here,
Though this is my start,
It isn't easy,
Is this clear?

Hunger

I was starving,
I could hear my tummy rumbling,
I was distracted in class,
By the hunger I was feeling,
Then along came my savior,
In a hoodie so black,
I was shocked but glad when she had my back,
She gave me a cookie,
Yes a cookie it's true,
A cookie of black and white too,
The chocolate outside was the first taste i had,
Though the creamy inside made it not bad,
I'll never regret this friend that i made,
Cause Alli gave me a cookie and that made my day.

(dedicated to Alli who gave me oreos in the library)

There's no meaning to this

There's a girl that i know &
She ages quite slow.
There's a dog down the road &
He once ate a toad.
There's a stranger in my dreams &
I don't know what it means.
But I do know this &
My rhyming skills are good.

Breathe

I closed my eyes to catch my breath,
But I'm not sure what happened next,
The beeping has stopped,
The lights went out,
The people are crying,
I can't figure it out.

#Shakespeare

To thine own self be true,
And to thine own self you'll prove;
That thine own self is better than else,
So please just be thine own self.

Home

There's a place I know if you're looking for a home,
It's got a bed and a door;
Of that i'm quite sure,
Where You sleep at night is an important decision,
So here I am to make a suggestion;
You could buy this one and get a free rug,
I promise-I promise I got out all the bugs;
There isn't a chance you'll buy it, is there?
Well that okay, I have till the door to make you hear,
Here on the wall I washed off the blood,
Of that awful time when we carved the pig good,
And this dent here was from a body,
My sister sure didn't like that doll Bobby,
She said he was scary,
And coming alive,
I'm not sure i believe it,
I'm sure it's a lie,
She hid it in the attic,
Here come, I'll show you,
Just watch your head,
Don't want to lose you too,
Don't take it like that!
I didn't mean death,
It's just that well,
You'd never guess.

See now that I have trapped up here,
I can finally tell you about what you fear;
You were right when you started,
You will probably die,
Don't worry I won't kill you,
Probably suicide,
He does that to all of them,
So I'm sorry I lied,
But it's your problem now,
So I guess this is goodbye,
And well who knows,
Maybe you'll survive.

College

College is like an ocean with tons of fish,
But I'm the shy one who just can't swim;
It's like a bee hive with too much honey,
But I'm the poor bee with allergies.

It's like kindergarten before all your friends,
Nobody told me I'd have to do this again;
It's like when you first joined a team,
I'm the kid who has no one to pass with.

College is big, it's vast, and confusing,
I had hoped there would be more weight I was losing;
There are times when people just stand and stare,
And i spend hours wondering what's there.

Do you remember that time you made your first friend,
And remember what happened just then?
I remember and it's making me sad,
Why did no one tell me that when it comes
to making friends I'm bad.

College is hard, it's stressful, and frustrating,
I don't think they know how much money I'm making;
I'm not very good at it though no one's surprised,
It would appear I've reached my full potential in their eyes.

College is like swimming but not knowing how,
So all you can do is try not to drown;
I don't know if I'll make it, but baby I'll try,
It'll take more than this to make me cry.

Art

Art is expression,
In various forms,
It's using your talent to make weird things the norm.

Art is expression,
Of emotions it's true,
It's using colors to make blue more than blue.

Art is expression,
But it's more than paint,
It's using an instrument to open a gait.

When a person does an art,
It's different for each;
Because while mine is this part,
Yours could be to teach.

Art is important though,
And this part I mean;
It's an expression of just who we are as human beings.

Page 21

This is page 21,
It's not the best page,
It didn't even run,
But it's my favorite page you see,
Because this is the page where you meet me,
This is the page about all my secrets,
The ones that no one knows I am keeping,
Once I have said them you'll know who I am,
But please don't worry,
No one else can,
So Nikki likes Jacob but he doesn't know,
And Julia wants a divorce,
Her husband has got to go,
Jamie snuck out,
But didn't get caught
She never will,
I might have been bought,
Collin will propose,
Though even he doesn't know,
And me?
Well i don't have a secret about me,
Everything is open,
Out there to see,
I'm a barista and make coffee,
I'm in college and just barely passing,

But that's okay,
Who really cares,
I'm sure I will one day,
But that days not here,
If you really wanna know,
Then here i go,
My name isn't my name,
And that is quite so,
See I've changed it you see,
Into something else,
The Castle it is,
Isn't quite it,
I won't tell you though,
Somethings i've got to keep,
Because these aren't my secrets you see,
But they are mine to keep.

Unique

People are different,
In more ways than one,
Sometimes they walk,
But sometimes they run.
Sometimes they move with their heads held high,
And sometimes they move like they want to cry.
Sometimes they skip,
To a beat of their own,
Or sometimes they don't,
They just move alone.

Trust

I'm not a good writer,
And I don't know how to sing,
But someone has to say it,
So I hope you're listening.

Humans are cruel,
We destroy what we touch,
I'm sure that's why God,
Didn't trust us with much.

But a future is coming,
Where he might have to try,
Because the future is ours,
To live or to die.

Belief

No one is coming,
We're not being saved,
Depression is crushing us,
Wave after wave.

But I believe in people,
In the kindness we hold,
I'll believe we'll save us,
Be brave, be bold.

The Path

There's dust on my feet and wind in my hair
But at this point I've decided not to care
I walk this path by the ocean so blue
But I'm never alone there's me and there's you
So here I go down these steps again
Here I cross at this riverbend
Here I came to the decision
That sometimes the mountains we see
Decide who we'll be

Scared

There pictures on her skin
And metal in her face
Her clothes im sure
Have been in a better place
Her knuckles are torn
She's running out of breath
I can tell she's scared to death.

Author

My wrist hurts,
My head is pounding;
I have six more pages,
So yeah I'm frowning.

But time will pass,
Aches will fade;
I'll get finished,
Just maybe not today.

I worked my ass off,
To get this far;
No one ever told me,
Writing was so hard.

Sure the words are easy,
And the story flows;
But as I write,
My pain just grows.

My hand will cramp,
And my words will stutter;
I don't know how,
To make the story better.

I'll add a villian,
Maybe a hero or two;
But then you have to name them,
And nothing will do.

Next you try horror,
Thinking scary is easy;
But as your characters bleed,
You start to get queasy.

There really isn't a way,
To make your story great;
It take frustrated tears,
Just to write one page.

But you're trying so hard,
And writing so much;
That you're starting to think,
You might have the touch.

As you reach the end,
And your story unfolds;
You ignore all others,
And focus on your goal.

You've decided on the cast,
On the storyline too;
Now there's only one thing left,
and you know what to do.

Give your readers an ending,
One they'll never forget;
Introduce a new character,
Or a character's death.

Make it something,
That brings them back;
And then close the book,
With a resounding crack.

Now that you've finished,
You're shaking with fear;
And if nobody likes it,
You don't want to hear.

You've written so much,
And dug so deep;
That you put your soul in it,
Out for the world to see.

You can't take it back,
And wouldn't if you could;
Because this is just the beginning,
It's only the first book.

My Message

I'm flying through the air,
And you probably don't care,
But i'm saying goodbye from here.
I'll text my goodbye,
From my seat in the sky,
And check your reply on landing.
And my message will say,
In words my way that,
"I'm leaving, as you read this,
I'm soaring across the sky.
Soon I'll be home again,
So this is goodbye."

I'm crushed in a seat,
Finding it hard to breathe,
There's stuff i regret,
And i didn't want to leave.
To cry from the clouds,
But i couldn't stay,
So I got lost in the crowds.
I won't check my phone until I touch down,
Cause looking right now would mean turning around.
So just read my text, and I'll think it too,
It says,
"I'm leaving, as you read this,
I'm soaring across the sky,
Soon I'll be home again,
So this is goodbye."

As I sit here between two strangers,
I think about our meeting and how we arranged it.
I think about the club where you danced and twirled,
I think about my friends that you loved and adored.
Looking back now i can tell it wasn't me,
When you spun over I all but dropped to my knees.
Your beautiful smile that shines like the sun,
And your beautiful hair I wanted to touch.
I don't know why you chose me,
Or how we ever worked,
But sitting here now these are my words,
"I'm leaving, as you read this,
I'm soaring across the sky.
Soon I'll be home again,
So this is goodbye."
Goodbye.

Secret

The secret to shakespeare,
Is really quite obvious;
He likes to kill his characters,
And give them sad deaths.

So when you're reading Shakespeare,
Don't expect a happy ending;
Honestly it would be unusual,
If they lived past the beginning.

He stabbed Julius Caesar,
Sent Romeo to his death;
Drove Hamlet insane,
Let's not even mention Macbeth.

So "Lay on MacDuff",
Pierce my "too, too frail skin";
And then "lend me your ears",
While he tears us apart.

Here lies Tiffany

Now i lay me down to sleep,
I pray the lord my soul to keep;
May angels watch me through the night,
And wake me in the morning light.

If in the morning I do not wake,
I pray the lord my soul to take;
Tell my family I went and died,
Though I'm happy, so do not cry.

I said my prayers, and made my choice,
I know my path, we must rejoice;
If this does come to pass,
Bury me in a field of grass.

My soul is safe up above,
I watch them now with faith and love;
On my headstone written in tears,
It says, "Here lies Tiffany, young in years".

She left us here though we do not weep,
She went above his soul to keep;
She watches through the night,
And wakes us in the morning light.

Though if one night we do not wake,
We pray the lord our souls she takes;
Tell our friends we went and died,
We found our daughter, do not cry.

On a stone, in a field,
It was written in stone with steel;
"Here lies a family, whole and free,
They are finally together, be happy".

Math

I promise I'm smart,
I swear it's true;
But this is math,
And I haven't a clue.

Short

This one is short,
And quite sweet;
I like George,
But he likes meat.

Duck

I'm still bad at dancing,
My singing skills suck;
But I know where I'm going,
And you look like a duck.

Soulmates

I've met someone special,
We're taking our vows,
It's only been a week,
But we now own a house.
We're staying together,
Through all types of weather;
Our children are plenty,
Though my favorite is Emily.
Time is passing,
But our love never fades;
We were meant for each other,
See, we're soulmates.

Gone

My fingers are shaking,
I'm dripping with sweat,
My stomach is churning,
And we only just met,
A new sun is rising,
The days go on,
But i blinked my eyes,
And now you're gone.

Sorry

My knees hit the floor,
My hands come together,
All i want is one day more,
Not to party or play you see,
But one whole day for you and for me,
So i'll send him some words,
They say it takes faith,
I might just break,
I'm sure i look awful,
Since my hair's all gone,
My skins turning yellow,
It's time to move on,
Please don't hate me,
For taking control,
I knew what came next,
I'm not on my own,
I have some family here,
Wherever 'here' is,
And i knew my options,
before leaving there,
So wipe your tears,
Pick up your body,
Conquer your fears,
And find somebody,
I know it's not easy,
I know you're sad,
But now isn't the time,
To not be glad,

Because i chose this,
It was all me,
So take this time,
To just believe,
Believe in me,
In the choice i made,
It's what i wanted,
It's better this way,
I'm sorry of course,
For the pain that you feel,
I know you wish,
This wasn't real,
I know you dream,
Of a life for me,
I know you pray,
That i'm happy,
So this is me,
Laying your fears to rest,
I'm going now,
It's for the best.

Family

Kelsie is blonde,
She's pretty and tall;
She has those eyes,
For which you could fall.
Ryan is smart,
He's giant and brave;
He's the type of person,
For which you would crave.
I am short,
I'm quiet and observant;
I tend to use sarcasm,
As a solid defense.
This is my family,
We're different us three;
But we love each other,
As you can see.

Dear Brother

I know you're angry,
And rightfully so,
I probably should have told you,
Before the show,
But the truth is this,
And i'll spare no details,
So listen close,
To my woes and my fails,
I never once lied,
About how i felt,
I told you i cried,
About how i fell,
I told you his name,
But no, not his age,
But try to convince me,
You wouldn't do the same,
So yes, we kissed, we played, we missed,
But no, i didn't tell you this,
It was a secret you see,
Something we kept,
Between him and me,
I get why you're mad,
Trust me, i do,
But i couldn't tell you,
Until our relationship grew,
I wanted security,

To have faith in our love,
But looking back now,
I don't think there was,
I know my own feelings,
And i trust my heart,
But i don't this his ever wanted to part,
He liked the big moments,
A little too much,
He expected a lot,
Just before lunch,
You're so happy,
And i wanted that too,
So i straightened my back,
But his expectations grew,
I couldn't meet them,
Since i'm still just a kid,
And with every failure,
His anger got big,
At first i was mad,
I yelled and i fought,
But quickly i learned,
To just hide a lot,
Today was a surprise,
I didn't see coming,
But here i am now,
Crying and bleeding,

I'll probably die from this,
The stab wounds are deep,
I secretly hope,
You kill this creep,
I know thats wrong,
But it's my dying wish,
Avenge my death,
Don't let him live,
This is my story,
I hope you're not sad,
I love you big brother,
p.s. - be mad.

Us

Shining like the sun,
Quiet like the night;
We've only just begun,
I'll try to treat you right.
Let's lay here together,
Let's whisper to each other;
Let's waste our lives away,
Promise not to move all day.
I could spend a lifetime,
Stuck in your eyes;
I love that in the daylight,
They show what's inside.
If this is all i get,
I'm quite content;
If this is all we are,
We'll go quite far.

What are you doing?

First your right,
Then your left;
Moving faster,
You're not tired yet.

Bring it up,
Set it down;
Feel the rhythm,
Hear the sound.

Take a breath,
Pause right here;
Then keep going,
The end is near.

Now it's over,
You did your best;
You showed something,
I'll never forget.

Little Sister

She's blonde,
She's strong,
She's seen every version of "Bring It On",
She prays,
She's brave,
She'll conquer hearts with just a wave,
So no, I'm not worried,
I don't need to stress,
Because my little sister,
Is already the best.

Life

Smell the leaves in the air,
Feel the wind through your hair,
Let the sun touch your face,
Feel the burn in it's place,
Let the rain wash away,
All the things you fear this day,
Don't be sad, do not weep,
This is your chance to leap,
Please be brave,
Ignore the grays,
Do your best to spend your time,
Up and far from mine.

Memory Lane

First things first,
you were promised a rap,
And don't freak out,
We'll get to that.
Before that though,
We have a score to settle,
About those times,
You started to mettle,
We'll start with our past,
Of the time i spent in a cast,
Of your obstacle courses we ran,
And all that time stepping on cans,
Of the poor little hamster,
That I'm sure you forgot,
Or that mean little boy,
That for me, you fought,
Do you remember when the swimming pool froze,
Or back when mom planted that rose?
What about swimming in the yard,
Or all those games we played in the car?
My favorite was the one,
Where you were a judge,
Though looking back now,
It doesn't seem like much,
You worked really hard,
to keep us busy,

I'm fairly sure now,
It wasn't too easy,
I wanted to thank you,
For attention you gave me,
I wanted to tell you,
That I'll always love you,
Since I'm not good with people,
And I'm definitely not Kelsie,
I'll do this instead,
Of embarrassing us slightly,
I hope that you like it,
And find it acceptable,
Because this is your present,
And it's non-refundable.
(For my big brothers wedding, I love you Ryan)

Lion

I felt time stop,
And my heart stood still;
Everything inside me started to drop,
Tears fell against my will.
The Puppy cried,
She couldn't understand;
And after catching my mind,
I gave her my hand.
The Rhino stood frozen,
His blood running cold;
Wondering what happened then,
Nothing being told.
The most unnerving one,
The one that brought us fear,
Is the Gorilla who wasn't here;
He was with the Lion who lost her roar,
Who wouldn't be the same anymore.
I don't know who told the forest about our pain,
And I don't know who helped me up again;
All I know is that it was the Cat who help my hand.

Words are Repeating

There are words repeating in my head.
And creepy crawlies under my bed.
There are things at home I've still not done.
And yet somehow all my time is gone.
There video game pets I'm sure are dead.
And words are repeating in my head.
There are mistakes I made as a child.
And a long time back I read the Bible.
There are books I own but haven't read.
And words are repeating in my head.
There was a time I owned a horse.
And ran a homemade obstacle course.
There's a place where my tears are shed.
Are words are repeating in my head.

Destiny

My minds flung from place to place,
My heart is strung by fates lace;
My soul was beaten by hells fury's,
And my life was woven to be buried.
My hope is smashed by the famous one,
My failings trashed like I have none;
My path was woven on the loom of fate,
That's why it is not you I hate.
Suppose I quit and went my own way,
Suppose it was not me chosen that day;
Would you still love the way you do,
Or would you hate and kill a few?

Take a Deep Breath

Take a deep breath, Step back,
Look again, And then begin.
No one is judging your progress,
No one is hoping you fail,
We're waiting at the top,
And I know you'll prevail.
This is your fight, But I swear to help,
This is not war, It is a duel,
Between you and yourself.
Every time you trip,
Every time you fall,
Just remember,
Take a deep breath, step back,
Look again, and then begin.
I promise to catch you,
I promise to wipe your tears,
I promise that when this is over,
I'll l comfort your fears.
You have to realize this on your own,
You have to see how much you've grown.
So I'll tell you the only thing I can,
Take a deep breath, step back,
Look again, and then begin.

My Story

I live in a world of sunshine,
But the world is full of grays,
And to accept that I needed to get out of the rays.
So wait for my time,
I'll make you mine,
So make up your mind,
About my sunshine.
I don't have a sob story,
My family is great,
They love me even though I'm perpetually late.
I don't like violence,
I fight with sarcastic snarks,
So excuse me for my rude remarks,
I tend to use silence and a form and suspense,
I like that my fake kindness is seen as good intent,
I like to watch and judge your actions,
It's almost like everyone has their own captions

Hurts

I wanna scream so bad it hurts,
But all the words are stuck in my throat;
I wasn't ever taught how to be this person,
I have no idea how to make this work.
I'm not happy with how this turned out,
I wanted something a bit more;
I have a lot of doubts,
But we'll see what's in store.

Dear Big Sister

I hope you know I love you,
And that I know you love me too;
That being said you must realize,
He's not the type to be nice.
I know he will hurt you,
I know you'll let him too;
I've just myself started to realize,
That you don't want him to be nice.

Breydon

I'm haunted by a ghost,
It's a little boy called Breydon;
He steals my emotions sometimes,
But he's the only reason I'm alive.

My Fears

Cold little fingers wrapped around my wrist,
Big green eyes covered in mist;
Long blonde hair turning red,
These are the fears in my head.
Strong, broad shoulders shaking in pain,
Bubbling emotions impossible to tame;
Wonderful siblings lying dead,
These are the fears in my head.

Praise

Let me take a moment to sing some praise,
Though it's not for anyone else these days;
My mom taught me endurance,
To never give up;
My dad taught me compassion,
To sometimes look up.
my brother gives me strength,
He holds me up tall;
My sister gives me courage,
To fight no matter what falls.

To My Kitty

I like to watch you dance,
To witness you take a chance;
I like to watch you grow,
I'm extremely proud, ya know;
As the years roll by and you advance,
Remember, I like to watch you dance.

Savior

It's because the things I've done in life,
That I can see you now;
Standing there above us all,
And never looking down.
We are equal in your eyes,
And of that I am proud;
I know what awaits us soon,
But I also know you'll be the savior of this town.

Help

Speak the words you keep in your heart,
Smile at the people who frown;
Keep your anger to yourself,
And never let others fall down.
You're the one left standing,
You're the one holding the torch;
No one else is helping,
Though of course you won't be forced.
You could just watch if you want,
You could let the world burn;
Just step back and keep quiet,
And let the page turn.
Or you could scream,
You could reach out your hand;
You could feed the ones who are hungry,
Do anything except just stand.

Letter Goodbye

I'm secretly hoping that I don't know you,
That you don't recognize my name;
I don't need the judgement that comes with that,
Of the unwanted fame.
I'm really hoping we're not related,
And that you won't see me on the street;
I don't want you to know my secrets,
That's not what I need.
So please don't try to discover my secrets,
Or to unravel my words;
I really don't want anyone to know me,
To know what I'm working towards.
This is the only book I'll do like this,
Cause this was fucking hard;
It's super easy to run out of rhymes,
And you end out putting random words like card.
So for my next book I'll do something different,
I'll make it a story I guess;
Or something else,
It'll probably not be my best.
There is some good in this though,
Cause when you're writing poems;
You're in charge,
And you're never wrong no matter what you do.

About the Author

Ismene Cook is the author of Oranges, when they are not writing they enjoy reading, spending time with family and listening to music. They've spent many years working on a series of books they can't wait for everyone to see and enjoy.